MARCHING ORDERS
Establishing a Strong Kingdom Perspective and a Mission Mindset

Frank Vega Jr.

MARCHING ORDERS
by Frank Vega Jr.

Printed in the United States of America

ISBN 1-60034-733-9

www.xulonpress.com

Dedication

This book is dedicated to all the suffering people of the world. Especially to the little orphans affected by HIV/AIDS, some of whom I have personally held and touched with the love of Christ.

To the Liberian Orphan Project and Malawi compassion project. I pray that through World Wide Compassion Organization, we can touch many lives and let the suffering know that their Father in heaven loves them much more that we can ever love them.

To Chuck Lewis and Family, who have been Angels sent by God. I love you very much.

TABLE OF CONTENTS

Acknowledgments

⸻

I want to first give thanks to God for saving and restoring my life, for imparting unto me His true purpose for my life—to share His compassion with a hurting, needy and dying world. No other treasure has been more valuable to me than this God-given assignment to pursue this work of compassion.

To those who are my greatest sources of support:

My wife Carmen, a woman of strength, wisdom, and character. Thank you for always being there, even through the hard and difficult times.

My children, Lavorn, Pastor Jose, Judith, Julius, Felicita, Frankie, their mates Shannon, Debora, Melissa, Fred and Ben. You have been by my side from day one through good and bad times. You continue to sacrifice daily to help me to pursue His mission and vision of compassion. I love you all unconditionally and totally.

My grandchildren, Genesis, Judith, Amber, Dominique, Nina, Micah, Amiri, Alexa and Jeremiah. You have helped me to really learn to be the father

I am today. I love you all with all my heart. Thank you.

To Rev. Doug Rogers of Teen Haven, a man who impacted my life during my gang days in Philadelphia—the only Caucasian guy in the sixties who would serve in the midst of the inner city street violence. You really loved and believed in us gang members.

To Rev. Melvin Floyd, a Godly man who continues to pour out his life for the lost. He impacted my life at the age of 12 through a can of soda and a soft pretzel when I was hungry and going to jail. Thank you Lord for our friendship today.

To Rev. James McKee and family. Thank you for your friendship and for being a spiritual father and role model to me.

To Rev. Terry Roach and family. Our trip to Israel bonded us together as brothers for life.

To Bishop Gilbert Coleman my spiritual father, for allowing me to be part of what God purposed for the Kingdom. I am very grateful for what I have learned from you.

To Dr. Willie Richardson for being an encouragement and building me up when I preached. You are part of why this book has become a reality. Thank you.

To Denise Short of Selah Transcription Services, Biblia Kim, Patricia Orozco, Rebekah Chang and Sara Chang for all your hard work and time spent on the transcript and final editing. Thank you for inspiring and encouraging me.

To all the great people from the streets, villages, and colonias who let me love, hug, and understand their conditions, suffering and pains.

To Urban Worship Center, Inner City Missions, and now World Wide Compassion Organization. Through the years we have cried, rejoiced, labored, learned and grown together. I am who I am today— a man of compassion—because of you. The Lord bless you.

Foreword

————∞∞∞————

The greatest component of any person's life is that they discover why God created them; undoubtedly this has happened in the life of Frank Vega. Frank is a passionate man who has wholeheartedly given himself over to the one true passion of his life — — winning souls to the Kingdom of God. In this book he has captured God's heart and his own by expressing the fact that today's Christian is often remiss in fulfilling our obligation to the Lord by being a witness no matter where we are. Very rarely is a person as transparent as Frank, but, nonetheless he has completely bared his soul so that all can see that if God can change him He can change anyone.

The world is in total disarray and confusion at present and it is up to the many believers in Christ to show a lost and dying world that there is hope in Jesus Christ. This book will give the reader the tools necessary to become more proactive instead of reactive to the conditions of the world. I have known Frank for many years and his love for the Lord and for winning souls is unwavering. Marching Orders is a stern challenge to every believer to develop the same passion as Frank, whether you witness in the inner city, the suburbs, or in the jungles of Malaysia. At present there are at least 6.3 billion people on planet earth; of those people it is estimated that at least 3.1 billion people have not heard the gospel. This is an indictment against the church because it says we have yet to heed to the last command of Jesus as He was making His way back to glory; "Go into all the world and make disciples." After this book let it stir your heart to witness every opportunity you have, and to spread the gospel to all who will receive it. I am certain that this book will ignite a blaze within your heart to receive the challenge of Jesus, but also to receive Frank's challenge and win the world for Jesus Christ!

Bishop Gilbert Coleman
Freedom World Wide Covenant Ministries

MARCHING ORDERS

Focus on the Cross

B ill Bright, the founder of Campus Crusade for Christ often says, "If coming to know Christ is the greatest thing that has happened to you, it only makes sense that the greatest thing you can do for someone else is introduce them to Him." As you come to have a more intimate relationship with Jesus, you'll come to know more of Him, His desires, His will, and His purpose for you, and you will want to tell somebody else that the living God wants to do the same thing for them. On the job tomorrow, at the office, you should be excited, running in to tell them about what God has revealed to you. And if they aren't saved, you need to tell them about Christ right there.

In 2 Corinthians 5:14-15, the attitude of channeling our gratitude into faithful and loyal obedience to Christ is addressed:

For Christ's love compels us, because we are convinced that one died for all, and therefore all died. And he died for all, that those who live should no longer live for themselves but for him who died for them and was raised again.

Do you understand your marching orders? It's not about us, but about Christ and the cross. Realizing that Jesus died for our sins and accepting that death forever changes our attitude about life and about ourselves. That is what it has to do to us, for once we understand that, it changes our attitude about everything, because the center is now about Christ.

Don't Give Up

What happened when Jesus hung on the cross almost 2,000 years ago to set man free for eternity? You've got to get people to understand this, and you cannot give up on them. When they say they don't want to hear it, keep trying. The Bible says not to grow weary in well-doing, for in due time you will reap a harvest. The farmer does not reap right away, continuing to plant, water, and cultivate with patience, because there is a process to the harvest. We don't have any patience; we want to see McDonald's-type fast food salvation. But it does not work like that, which is why we get discouraged so quickly. We need to have patience, and if we don't have it, we need to pray and ask God for it, because it takes a lot of loving.

It took a lot of loving and a lot of praying for me to come to Christ. I had my grandmamma, who was 109 years old when she died. She was a slave to the Spaniards in Puerto Rico, and used to sit there chewing tobacco or smoking a cigar with a rag wrapped around her head. But she prayed for me because I was the black sheep of the family, the one who gave my mother all the problems. But I had a grandmother who prayed for me all the time, even when I went to prison. Instead of giving up on me, she always told me that I would one day go on to touch people's lives- something I never forgot. She always told me not to worry about what I was going through, and advised me, "Son, just be yourself; be yourself," even when she knew I was going through addiction at the age of 11. After my grandmother refused to give up, and through all the prayers and loving, it became true, not to boast in myself.

You are very important to every person out there who is living a crisis life because, for some, the only Jesus that they will ever see is you. So we've got to have patience, and if we do not have it, we need to pray for it, because it is a process and takes time.

It took 23 years of my life. I remember the brothers from Teen Haven, including Doug Rogers, a man who influenced my life as the only white guy who would come into the city in the midst of gangs, and set up shop on Susquehanna Avenue just to love us gang members. He used to throw me out of Teen Haven every other night, but he continued to love me. Today, when I attend pastors' and leaders' meetings, he is also there, and I feel so good as I say, "Lord, thank you for him. Thank you for not letting him give up on me. Thank you for him who continued to love me when I didn't want to be loved." I thank God for even the seeds that he planted which other people watered throughout the years. 23 years later, God gave the increase.

Our Duty and Privilege to Follow Christ

That is why we cannot give up. We must obey Him and take the liberated message of the cross to the world. We need to stop being selfish with this, because it is not our message, it is His. We have been given the obligation, and the privilege, to serve the King of Kings and the Lord of Lords. That is the motivation! We do it because it has been directed by Jesus Christ, as He said, "Go and make disciples of all nations." He did not say to worry about your problems or to think it was all about you. Rather, He said, "With the same love that I love you, love your brother; love your sister," whether they are saved or not.

God loves even the sinner, so what is our problem? Why do we not love the sinner until we see increase in their lives? He loved us, but we forget where we came from and the comfort that He gave us. We need to give that love to somebody else.

When reading 2 Corinthians 5:14-15, people probably wonder why Paul decided to live like this. Simply put, Paul lived in such a way because Jesus lived that way. He willingly followed the path of the cross and identified with Christ by faith. In Philippians 3, Paul shares that everything that was prophesied to him in the past is now meaningless, garbage, because he has come to a new revelation. He has a new motive now, and he considers everything a loss compared to the surpassing greatness of knowing Christ. This man was willing to leave everything behind to know Christ, including his good education and his position as part of the elite society. He had no need for anything, but he counted it all loss for the surpassing knowledge of knowing Jesus Christ.

For us to know Jesus Christ, there are sacrifices to be made, and some roads that have to be traveled that we would rather not. There are some rivers and countries that we have to cross, some people that we have to love, that we don't want to cross or love.

But it is about the cross. If we are going to be obedient to God and call ourselves His servants, that is the focus. For us, the cross means coming to church every week, the cross means hugging a dirty individual or just sitting down with them and giving them a cup of coffee.

Following God's Orders

A Nigerian pastor friend of mine had the opportunity to go to Rome, but was wondering why God sent him there. As his friend picked him up and they went driving down the road, he started to see all the prostitutes, topless, lining up along side the road, and he started to understand why God had sent him there. There are prostitutes from Africa being sent to Rome, sold for $15,000, who earn $50 to $75,000 for pimps before getting their freedom. However, there was nobody in Rome at that time to reach the girls, some of whom were still virgins before being sold. Rome is a very religious city, and yet there are young ladies being sold into slavery right in front of their faces, and they will not rescue them.

My friend said, "Okay, God, this is what you want me to do, I'm going to do it ," and invited a prostitute to have a cup of coffee with him. As he talked with her, she broke down and cried, saying, "There is no way that I can be set free." However, he led her to Christ, and though he thought he would have some problems with her pimp, the pimp actually gave him money to start a church for the prostitutes in Rome.

All of this was possible because he was obedient to God and just went. He hopped on a plane, somebody met him there, and the pimp gave him money to get a house to start a church. Now, they are reaching prostitutes in Rome.

That is why Paul decided to take the path of the cross. He said that everything he had meant nothing to him, rather, wanting "...to know Christ and the power of his resurrection and the fellowship of sharing in His sufferings, becoming like Him to death." We skip over that part when we read Philippians because we don't want to suffer. But there is a responsibility for every Christian to help fulfill the Great Commission because we now have an understanding that it is okay to endure, since the morning always comes. No matter where God has positioned you, as a factory worker, an office worker, or a member of a ministry, you have this obligation. We have to seize the moment to be a witness for Christ.

The Everyday Witnessing Christian

We cannot be a Christian today in church and leave it at home tomorrow. We should be talking about God everywhere we go because it is about Him, and it is Christ who is in us. But so often, we leave our Christian character at home. We go to work and act just like the unsaved folks. But we need to use the positions that God has given us or placed us in to reach and disciple people; to tell them about Christ, that He loves them, and that He wants to change their lives.

You don't have to wait to go to the mission field, for your mission field is right outside of the four walls of the church. Right outside your door is your job, the factory, and the office, for on whatever land you set foot, it becomes holy ground. You do not have to go overseas. They do need you, but until God gives you enough faith to take the step to go there, you need to minister the gospel right where you at.

Witnessing is not an option, as Matthew 28 states. We need to get out of the mentality that we can choose whether we want to witness or not, because it is God's will for our lives. If you want to see God's blessing in your life, you better start witnessing. We no longer are of ourselves- we belong to Christ. He paid a price for us and what He asks of us is very simple- to go and tell somebody about Jesus Christ. What is so hard about that? Why is it that we have to take ten courses in evangelism, and still cannot know what God wants us to do?

Even the little child recognizes the fundamental aspect of witnessing. I once had my little unsaved nephew on my back, and he wanted to sing the Barney song, but my granddaughter told him he had to sing the Jesus song. When he asked how, the 7-year-old child replied, "Well, you've got to receive Him in your heart first." God said that we need to be like the little ones because the gospel is a simple gospel. As adults, we often make it difficult and blow it out of proportion; when we want to witness, we start preaching to them and giving them Bible lessons, but the Bible tells us that those who are not saved are not going to understand what you are talking about. Why are you going to give them a Bible lesson when all you need to do is exhibit the love of Christ? We can do this by just hugging them, encouraging them, and praying for them- that's how you witness to them.

Worshipping and Witnessing

Everything we do must be based on two objectives: worshipping God and witnessing for Him. Our responsibilities hang on the things that He commands us to do, not on what we want to do. Though we know a lot of scripture, shout a lot of 'Hallelujahs,' and love to worship inside of the church, we often have anxiety about witnessing. However, you cannot have one without the other, because worshipping means nothing if you are not following through in obedience to the second command to witness! In Matthew 16:13-18, Jesus stresses this point to His disciples.

When Jesus came to the region of Caesarea Philippi, he asked his disciples, "Who do people say the Son of Man is?" They replied, "Some say John the Baptist; others say Elijah; and still others, Jeremiah or one of the prophets." "But what about you?" he asked. "Who do you say I am?" Simon Peter answered, "You are the Christ, the Son of the living God." Jesus replied, "Blessed are you, Simon son of Jonah, for this was not revealed to you by man, but by my Father in heaven. And I tell you that you are Peter, and on this rock I will build my church, and the gates of Hades will not overcome it."

Jesus wanted His disciples to know that they were called to be a part of something much greater than any of them could imagine, so He took them on a little strategy retreat, and posed a seemingly simple question: "Who do people say that the Son of Man is?" Today, we would call that market-sensitive questioning, a method used by businesses to pick people's brains about a new product. I believe Jesus wanted them to discuss what the people were saying about Him and His ministry when He asked, "What are they saying on the streets about me? Who are they saying I am?"

It is not about how great of a job we think we're doing, but it is about what unbelievers are saying about us and our walk. Because we represent Christ, what they say about us, they say about Christ. The word I hear in the streets everyday is that church folk are all the same, whether they are black, white, green, or blue. They say Christians are the same as anybody else because we haven't kept our word. We promise people things out there just to make ourselves feel good, but we don't follow through; we are not consistent with our witnessing, going from spot to spot like a carnival that is here today and somewhere else tomorrow.

Consistency

We have developed relationships with drug addicts, not because I used to be one, or because I came from the streets, but because we were consistent. We were in their faces every Friday with something to eat, praying with them, encouraging them, and building trust, even to the point of us being allowed into crack houses and shooting galleries. In the same way, the church needs to build trust with the world and those who are unsaved. Again, that trust comes through keeping our word, for we are representing Christ, and Christ will not be mocked or made a liar.

We cannot see changes by just hopping from place to place, but we need to be consistent in concentrating on one area. I can want to reach the whole city, but I cannot do so by myself. However, I can network with other people while I claim one area that I will focus on. But we naturally want to be all over the place. Ted Koppel's Nightline special about the Badlands showed this, as they documented churches coming down to Philadelphia from as far as

Maryland to feed the drug addicts. Even though the people would be able to go back and say they were on TV, they didn't really do anything, because the drug addicts are still there. That is why the word on the street is that Christians are all the same, because we're doing things to make ourselves feel good, but not living to worship God and lift up His holy name to glorify Him.

Returning to Christ as the Focus

The disciples said in Matthew 16:14, *"Some say John the Baptist; others say Elijah; and still others, Jeremiah or one of the Prophets,"* when asked who the Son of Man was, but Peter's response revealed the essence of Christian belief when he said, *"You are the Christ, the Son of the living God."* Peter hit the nail right on the head, for the core of his confession was the expression, "the Christ, the Christ." "Christ" is the New Testament Greek word for the Old Testament word "Messiah," both of which meant "the anointed one." Peter had a revelation as to whom Christ really was- the anointed one who came to set the captives free.

We also need to understand who Christ is. Can you answer when somebody asks you what can He do for them? He is the Christ, the one and only Messiah; there will never be another. He is the everlasting God, God in the flesh, Son of the living God, all power and authority to accomplish His purpose in this world, and He has all authority in heaven and on earth. But other people will not know all this unless somebody shows or tells them of how Christ came to love and comfort them. We need to show them that He hugged them and can bring restoration in their lives, He is the everlasting God, one with the power to tell a lame man to get up and walk, and one with the authority to call a prostitute his 'daughter' when others wanted to stone her. Man cannot do that. The world can't do that. Only Jesus Christ the Messiah can do that.

Representing Christ

To take some steps of action, we must first obey Romans 12:1-2 when it says we need to present our bodies as living sacrifices. "Why?" you might ask. Our bodies are the visible representations of everything that we were, are, and ever will be. We represent Christ, and what He has done to and for us. We are the perfect example of who Jesus Christ is in our lives, in the way that I am an example to drug addicts in my area, because they knew me when I was a walking dead person with my heart beating so hard and so fast outside of my shirt because of drugs. And though I use to be an individual who was intoxicated 7 days a week, 24 hours a day, a human garbage can for drugs, others are able to see a new person. Drug programs, prison, and the world did not make me like this. Only Jesus Christ was able to transform me. That is why I want to represent Christ when others see me.

To tell you the truth, people do not always see Christ in me, because I'm not perfect. Sometimes I lose it when people steal from me, and I apologize to God because I react sinfully when I represent Him, like when somebody who I let stay in the mission after getting beat up stole my new drill. I said, "I'm tired of them stealing from God," and chased him with a club, but I felt so convicted afterwards and asked the Lord to forgive me. Thank God that we serve a forgiving God. We're human and we lose it, but I had to go through that episode for God to tell me, "Frank, I don't need you to fight my battles, whatever they steal from you. It's not them stealing, it's the devil stealing." God said He would give whatever the devil steals back to you seven times, and so I've had about seven drills after that, and though they've gotten stolen, it is fine because it comes with the environment.

God taught me a lesson through that incident that when people see me, they need to see Christ, not only through being a cleaned-up individual, but in my actions and reactions. But I have to continually present myself as a living sacrifice to Him because it is part of my marching orders- keeping this body in submission, holy and blameless before Him. A living sacrifice is everything that we were, are, and ever will be.

Loyalty to God

Another part of our marching orders as Christians is to declare our allegiance to God by fulfilling the Great Commission. We do so by witnessing and being a model of who He is in our lives. The Bible says, "Do not be conformed to this world," and so we cannot act like the world or do the things that it does. We may want to be around sinners to be a tool God can use to lead them to the saving knowledge of Jesus Christ, but we cannot go along with their plans.

Today, much of the church has become like the world, but we cannot reach people if this continues! God has given us a plan to reach people. Sometimes methods of sharing the gospel change over time, but the gospel is still the same: it's still about Jesus Christ and the cross. It is still about people acknowledging that they are sinners and confessing with their lips that Jesus Christ is Lord.

Do not let the world squeeze you into doing the things that they want you to do, because we do not have to be like the world to reach the world. We can be the unique individual that God has created us to be- ambassadors for Him. We have to surrender our lordship to the lordship of Jesus Christ and not to the dictations of this world.

Committing to Action

The third part of the marching order is to commit to action. Be transformed by the renewing of your mind. Solomon said, "As a man thinks, so he is." Transformation is the product of what we think about, and so we should think about mission and witnessing, continually renewing our minds to the word of God, not through the things the world is telling us to do. Then, we will see ourselves being committed, and that commitment being exhibited in our actions. Transformation is the product of what we think about, so we need to start thinking about witnessing, the cross, and lost souls.

Stop thinking about trying to out-do your brothers and sisters and getting more degrees. There is nothing wrong with degrees, but we waste more time learning than doing, and we die with a lot of learning and no doing. The time is short. I love you, and this is why I'm telling you this. I cannot bite my tongue for Jesus Christ, for the Bible says that it is the truth that will set us free. We need the truth. You don't need a pastor who is going to pacify you so you can stay here and pay your tithes and your offerings, because when you're gone, I'm pretty sure God will send ten faithful servants in your stead. I'm not into keeping people happy, but I'm about telling the truth. The truth hurts sometimes, but hey, it brings healing to us.

Let us dwell on the Great Commission, on trying to be nice to our neighbors, and on exhibiting to them who Jesus Christ really is. If a person is a hypocrite, nobody may know in the present, but he will eventually be exposed because his actions will tell the story. Don't sit up in church and be a hypocrite; don't tell people that you're doing something, and then not do it, because the Bible says that everything you do in the dark will come out into the light. David says in Psalms 119:11, "*Your word have I treasured in my heart that I might not sin against you. Your word have I treasured in my heart that I might not sin against you.*" His word is our guide to victory and to fulfilling the Great Commission in this life.

The Importance of Personal Study

There needs to be an excitement about being Christians, whether in times of rebuke, hardships, trials, tribulations, or even good times. God has so much to give to us, and it is free for our taking. In order to continue obeying God's marching orders, it is important to maintain a sense of purpose, as indicated in 2 Timothy 4:1-5:

> *In the presence of God and of Christ Jesus, who will judge the living and the dead, and in view of his appearing and his kingdom, I give you this charge: Preach the Word; be prepared in season and out of season; correct, rebuke and encourage—with great patience and careful instruction. For the time will come when men will not put up with sound doctrine. Instead, to suit their own desires, they will gather around them a great number of teachers to say what their itching ears want to hear. They will turn their ears away from the truth and turn aside to myths. But you, keep your head in all situations, endure hardship, do the work of an evangelist, discharge all the duties of your ministry.*

A lot of you may think that this passage is mainly for the pastors and leaders who will have to endure hardship and go through problems, but we need to apply them to our own lives if we want to continue to mature in Christ and be all that God has created us to be. If we do not study and stay in the word of God to seek Him

23

and the revelation of His word, we will be deceived, and are never going to believe what the pastor preaches from the pulpit. You aren't going to know if it's the truth or a lie. In our small church, I tell the congregation that I want them to go and make sure that what I preach lines up with the word of God. We need to study just as hard as the preachers.

The Importance of Purpose

I heard years ago that if you have a good why for living, you can stand through anything. If you have the right purpose, it will give you stability in your life by anchoring you in the hard times, even bringing you to edit your priorities. I'm talking about us personally putting ourselves before God as a mirror to find out what our priorities are, even before our brothers and sisters and allowing them to see through us, because sometimes, pleasing our human bosses seems more important than pleasing God.

But Paul brings out some awesome principles in 2 Timothy. He says if we build our lives on the wrong purposes, we can expect to experience aimless confusion and emptiness, wandering around the desert like the Israelites for forty years. This happened because they had no purpose, and if they did, it was the wrong purpose. Confused and not knowing what awaited them where God was leading them, they started grumbling and complaining, and Moses could not change their mentality. Only when they had the right sense of purpose, God's purpose, were they able to see where they were going. That is why many preferred to go back to Egypt, where there was plenty to eat. They would be in bondage, but it was better because they wouldn't have to make any commitments.

Commitment to Doing, Not Just Knowing

Commitment is a bad word in Christian circles. Nobody wants to make a commitment. I'll stay right here, warm the pew, and give my tithes and my offerings as nobody sees me. But God sees, and even before you had the thought, He was already looking at you.

One of the major problems of Christianity today is that Christians know so much but do so little. We have all the right information and even the correct theology, but we do nothing with it. It's a shame.

Thank God that He loves us and keeps giving us a chance like He did with the Israelites, even in the midst of our sins. God keeps giving them enough room to repent and change their lives, even blessing them, as they sin.

Start getting onto the right purposes. We have the right knowledge about God in His word and it still has no effect on us. We have Bible teachers teaching the word of God in Bible colleges who are not even saved. Knowledge about God is not going to do it. Rather, you need His wisdom, which comes through trials and hardships, when you start walking out that knowledge of God. It does not come from gaining knowledge, but from the application of what you learn while earning that degree that causes things to happen, because it makes you have a purpose.

I believe God is setting the stage for a new spiritual awakening and revival in this country, but is waiting on us, that we might submit ourselves as workmen, worthy to be used for Him. We need to be worthy to be sent to other parts of the world, to go to our neighbors, and tell them about God. He wants His people to make the choice to live out that life of purpose that has been given in Christ.

It is one thing to have something, but it's quite another to use it. If you have a beautiful car and never drive it, you cannot complain about not being able to get somewhere. It is entirely your own fault. You decorate a car on the outside with a beautiful paint job, but without a motor, all you can do is sit in it and look pretty. That is where the church is at today. We want to just dress up on Sunday and look nice. But we don't need to look pretty for God because He says He loves us just the way we are. He just wants you to be committed to go and minister the gospel of Jesus Christ to a dying world. He is not concerned about you dressing up for church, though there's nothing wrong with it. It is about doing our Father's will, because impressing people isn't going to get them saved.

God-given Characteristics for Uphill Battles

Paul was very concerned for Timothy, a young pastor in training. In the fourth chapter of 2 Timothy, Paul summarizes for Timothy what must be done practically to maintain his sense of purpose while living in ministry in a culture hostile to Christianity.

The number one principle that Paul gave Timothy was to concentrate on his uniqueness. God has given all of us something special to be used to reach somebody else who is lost or hopeless. There is something about you that allows you to just hold somebody's hand or speak the word of God and encourage and comfort them. I love when Paul talks about giving comfort to others in the same way that you have been comforted. We forget how God comforted us, or how He used others to comfort us, and we don't even have the time to do so for somebody else. But he tells us, "You have uniqueness about you. If you just push aside all that junk and pride you have, your neighbor will be able to see you for who you are. They will see Christ in you."

For you who are still praying about God sending them somewhere, you just need to trust in God and go because He says, "Go and make disciples of all nations." He didn't say to spend two years praying, because God doesn't need that much time to answer your prayers or raise your support- everything has already been ordained and predestined for you. If God called you to the mission field, don't worry about support, because God has already appointed and raised people to provide for you. So why fear? He knows your needs; He keeps account of every hair on your head; He knows your problem before you even encounter it.

Paul describes the condition of society to Timothy. He tells him about the uphill battles and pressure he will face. There are going to be some times when you will have to cry in your secret place. But fear not, for God said He would never leave or forsake you. Paul wanted Timothy to know the rejection that he was going to experience, just like how your pastor lets you know week after week, what you need to do to become more mature in Christ, to become more committed to Christ, this body, and the lost world out there. He let Timothy know that God didn't call him to a playground. Everyday, it's a battlefield. You aren't going out there to play basketball with a bunch of youth; I'm calling you to a battlefield. Everyday that we get up as Christians- not as Christians who only want to be there sometimes, but as committed Christians to Jesus Christ, we are battling for lives that hang in the balance every day. God is going to hold us accountable, just like He is going to hold me accountable for every child I preach to during sidewalk Sunday school. I encounter drug dealers who tell me, "Pastor if you don't get them, we will."

It's real, and we need to wake up and understand that the battle is for souls. It's not about going through things as we whine about ourselves. We need to start worrying about others. There are people dying right now outside the church doors, and nobody is there to reach them. Nobody is there to get them a cup of coffee and just tell them that Jesus loves them. Why is it so hard for us to do that? It doesn't take a lot. God didn't ask you to change them- He just asked you to sow a seed and water some. He said He'll take care of the rest, but we can't even do that.

Being Aware

The second principle that is part of maintaining a sense of purpose is being aware of your environment. Be sober in all things, because we need to know what is going on around us. In church while pastor is preaching, we know what everybody is wearing, but we're not aware of what's happening outside where people die right around us. People are living crisis lives everyday but we're not aware of it.

In the last sentence, "But you, keep your head in all situations, endure hardship, do the work of an evangelist, discharge all the duties of your ministry," Paul summarized for Timothy what he had to do; "You need to mind your P's and Q's. There's a lot of stuff happening around you, so keep your head tuned. Don't just go on trying to be a minister in the gospel when you're unaware of what's going on around you." God wants to use us in an area, but we need to be aware of the things He has put there. He has put neighbors next-door, but we've already judged them, thinking that they don't want God. Who are we to say that? We don't even know their names. Rather, ask what you can do for them, hug them, encourage them, and make a commitment to pray for them. A pat on the back doesn't cut it. I challenge you. We just want to find out information when we don't need it; we've got enough information. Find out what their needs are- how can you pray for them? How can you be a support to them? When you pray for missionaries, you might not be in the foreign country with them, but you can help to hold up their arms through prayer and support. So make sure that they lack nothing.

That's why I can't understand why some mission organizations or churches who send out missionaries that need to live from day to day, even when they can be supported. They made a decision for God to go outside of their comfort zones to other countries that don't want them there preaching the gospel of Jesus Christ, and while they are risking their lives, they have every right to worry when we send them empty-handed. But they are living by faith.

Be sober and be aware of what's going on around you. What's happening in these other countries? How many of you try to subscribe to magazines or go online to find out about the persecution that is taking place with our brothers and sisters in other countries? You don't have to know them to pray for them.

The word sober also implies the idea of urgency of life. There has to be urgency about this life, an urgency to give God not just some, but everything that we have. We have but one life and that is the life that He gave us when we came to Him and accepted Him as our Lord and our Savior. But this is it; either we're going to do everything that God has called us to do, or we are going to turn our backs on Him and go to hell. That's a real word, and hell is real. If we don't do our job, a lot of people are going there unnecessarily. Everybody wants to preach about heaven and its blessings, but nobody wants to preach about hell, but hell is just as real as heaven, and it's going to be full of people if we don't make a commitment to reach them.

To be sober also means to concentrate on your moment. This is your moment. God said to work while it is day, because when night-time comes, it is over. No more working- it's lights out. He's going to say, "I'm calling you in. Come on and stand before me, I want to see what you did while the lights were on, while it was daytime." All of us are going to be judged and will have to give an account.

We've got to pull out our entire God-given purposes into every moment and we can't slack off or get comfortable. We are living in a time when we have no time to look pretty or to sit back and relax. I am telling you God is coming tomorrow, because He said nobody knows the day or the hour, but He's going to come back like a thief in the night. Remember Y2K? It didn't mean anything to me; I didn't buy any water or flashlights. Everybody was asking, "Pastor, what are you doing about Y2K?" I'm giving food to the poor, I'm clothing those who don't have any, I'm comforting those who need comfort. My Father told me I would never beg for bread, so why am I going to spend money on generators? I told my wife, "Babe, we'll just light up the scented candles if the power goes out".

I'm praying that God will just take us through a little experience. There are people in other parts of the world who don't have any electricity or clean water to drink. The poor newborns in Mexico broke my heart. I got milk for them because their mother was giving them unsanitary water with flour in it to make the water look white. America has everything; we are a blessed nation. So I pray that we go through some uncomfortable times, because it's going to help us to depend more on God. It is going to help us humble ourselves and see ourselves for who we are.

Embracing and Enduring Suffering

The expectation of suffering is also key to maintaining your sense of purpose in Christ. There's that word. Suffer. But Paul tells Timothy to endure hardship. It's hard because nobody wants to. But hardships draw us closer to God, and bring about healing and maturity. We have to get to the point where we can trust God and embrace the hardships, because they mold and shape us to build character. They build integrity and cause us to humble ourselves before God. We have to welcome hardships because if we cannot, we are going to be no good for the king. He can't use us. Everybody wants to get right with God successfully from the start without going through difficulties, but it's the stuff in the middle between the start and finish that refines us like gold- gold that has gone through the fire to get all impurities removed

I embrace adversity because I got to the point where I had to stop whining. I know that if God allowed them to come, it was for a specific reason that would benefit me and better my purpose. We have all the right information and theology, but we just don't know what to do. When Christians face hardships, our reactions are sometimes worse than the world's. But by them, God personally develops and refines us so we can do all things. We can do all things through Christ who strengthens us, because it is not by our own intellect strength, but through the power of the Holy Ghost. God is causing us to do it.

Paul tells Timothy endure, like a long-distance runner. He has to exercise those muscles and needs to keep running and training because his body has to stay trim. In the beginning, the muscles get cramps, but when they start expanding and getting hard, the pain goes away, and you are able to run further. The lungs feel like they want to burst, but the runner keeps pressing on. Paul was doing the same, pressing on even when being beaten down, and he tells us, "Endure, for the morning will come."

My own little story while I attended Jones Junior High School, where I was on the track and cross-country teams. I had to fight my way in and out of school so I carried a little machete in my sweat suit. The runner's training wasn't just to run for the school, but also to help me get back on the other side of the railroad tracks when I got chased from school. It's funny now, but the training in cross-country helped me run a little faster than my pursuers by developing my lungs for the times I had to run from them 5-6 blocks nonstop. I'm pretty sure I probably clocked some records back in those days.

The runner trains like this everyday. His whole body feels like it's going to break down on him, but he knows he has to keep doing it because he will eventually reach that peak where every part of his body is just right. He knows he will be able to run any race. But the thing is that he goes through the same routine day after day. The race is only the test for the endurance that he has developed, and this endurance is going to determine whether he wins or not. The same thing applies to how we run this life's race- how we preach the gospel of Jesus Christ, how many people we tell about Christ regardless of the hardships that rise up, what people say about us, and the rejections we encounter everyday. We've got to keep running. Rejection hurts, especially when you know that the Savior is who they need, but you keep running, because the further you run, the less pain you feel.

In my case, I went in front of a judge after getting out of prison who told me, "Frank, you need to go into rehab." But I told him I didn't need therapy. I got a little religious, since I had already accepted Christ, and they labeled me the religious patient at Eagleville

Hospital. I was using God as a reason for not needing rehab, but when I got there, I submitted to the judge because I wanted to submit to God. I said, "God, whatever you want done, I know you have a purpose in it because I know it's going to benefit me." In rehab, I was the religious patient who witnessed about Jesus.

However, I was still using Jesus as a wall to keep me from dealing with some problems. I had some bitterness in me. I hated the Koreans because they had physically abused me while I spent two and a half years in their prison, I hated the whites because they made me run home everyday from school; I hated everybody. I hated myself, and had some issues to deal with even when I found God and knew about His love. So, when an unsaved therapist told me, "I wish I had a mirror to put in front of your face so you could see the Christian you are," I went off. That did it to me. They made me talk about those issues three times a day for seven days, but the pain lessened the more I talked. The more we run this race and endure the suffering, the less the pain because He brings healing to us. He is making you strong in the faith, enabling you to endure anything, so that even hell will have to back off.

The only time the enemy can play tricks on our mind is when we allow him to. I talk to brothers who are serving and loving God, but who say they are still recovering addicts after ten years. "I am a delivered addict; I've been delivered by the blood of Jesus Christ, but I am not recovering." That is an abomination to Jesus Christ. For anyone in recovery- check yourself, because the last I heard or read, our God is a God of deliverance who sent forth His word and healed me of my disease. I became a new creation, whole again, when I turned to Him.

But it doesn't stop there, because even though I was a new creation, something was wrong. I was still thinking and doing some things like I used to. But God gave me a revelation, saying, "Frank, all you have to do now is start working on your character." That's the reason why I couldn't go into a crack house and minister to crack addicts for five years because I still needed to deal with some issues and make some adjustments in my character. We need to develop the character of Christ to line up with the new creation that we are. Now, I can go in crack houses, and they can blow smoke all in my face, but I've been delivered by the blood of Jesus Christ and set free in His name. You have, too. Just endure, stand fast, and know that God is able to do for you exceedingly and abundantly more than you or your feeble mind can imagine, speak, ask, or do. That is why I get excited about the word of God. He has done so much for me.

I tell people that if God doesn't bless me anymore, I'm content with it, for He has already blessed me so much. First of all, He's given me back my life which the enemy tried to steal from me. He's given me my family back, He's given me a ministry, and He's given me the strength to be able to endure the hardships that I face. Many of you are going through the wilderness today. But you take your wilderness and embrace it. When you come out on the other side, you'll never be the same. The pastor won't have to bug you or make you feel uncomfortable about coming to church, because you'll be the first one entering that door, and you'll probably stay for two services. You'll know that you know that you know that you know. That is why we have to learn to endure hardships.

The Focus on the Cross

Focusing on the core of the cost, the cross, is the fourth step to practically maintaining a sense of purpose in this culture. Paul said, "Timothy, forget about all this other stuff. I want you to focus on the cross." The cost for us is the cross of Jesus Christ, because that is where everybody is set free, and where everybody is healed, delivered, and restored. Why? Because it was all done at the cross. Missionaries should know that everything they go through today has already been completely done away with at the cross of Jesus Christ. You don't have to worry about it. All you have to do is endure and remember that you have to focus on the cost, the cross of Jesus Christ.

I get the feeling that brother Timothy probably wasn't a gifted evangelist, just like many of us aren't the best. But it is the enemy who puts that thought in our minds, and I believe that that is what keeps us from being witnesses for God. "Well, I don't know how to approach or speak to somebody." Years ago, I didn't know how to read well, and even now, I don't know how to speak very well, but I just want to be like Moses and encourage you. It's fine if you can only tell somebody that Jesus loves them. That's all He expects from you, for He didn't say that you had to use big words. All you have to do is just be yourself. It's fine if a lot of us are like Timothy; God is not holding that against us. But He will hold it against us if we are not committed, not sharing His gospel, or not exhibiting His love to those that need it.

In the hands of the master, you will be able to do anything that you put your mind to do for Christ. The Bible says that you can do all things- you can witness, you can pray for people, you can go to another country, you can support a missionary- through Christ who strengthens you, even when the feeble mind tells you that you can't. So why worry about it? Aren't we in the master's hands? Let's get up and go; let's minister to our neighbors. Let's get up and support our missionaries. What we don't have and we want to give, He'll make sure we get it to give it. I love that. I love to give. I tell the homeless guys and the drug addicts to give. We have a big five-gallon water jug, and I tell them to start giving, even if you only have two cents. I tell them to put an assignment on every penny they put in it, because it's a seed that is being sown- if you want God to deliver you out of drug addiction, put a few pennies in there and believe that He is going to do it. I'm teaching them to give from their heart, and to give freely even when they don't possess.

So Paul reminds his young friend not to forget the core of this thing called Christianity- the cross of Jesus Christ. He wants Timothy to make sure, that along with all of his other activities, like when we're washing our cars, dealing with our little idols, and the ladies go shopping, that he is keeping his focus sure. He is saying that when things need to be done in the church, and when people need to come and pray, they are still valid activities, but we're too focused on them, so don't forget what the cost is. It's about the cross. Don't get caught up in all that, but keep up in your commitment to what you been called to do.

Faithfulness and Obedience

Pursue faithfulness and obedience, and fulfill your ministry. Paul tells Timothy, "Look, don't draw on any personal fulfillment from the ministry, because it's not about that." If you are in ministry or in missions because you want people to look at you for doing that, God's not going to bless you, because you're in it for yourself. When I'm in ministry, it's not about Frank feeling good, because hardships don't make you feel good. I embrace it and I keep running with that, and when I pray for people, sometimes the spirit of God comes down on me and I cry like a baby.

I don't have any problems crying. A lot of us men need to put down our walls and be real. It's okay to be emotional, because in those tears, God purges some things out of us. We need to stop being those macho men. We know who we are, so let's just step in our proper position. If God created the man to be the head, then we should be that and not something that we aren't. And when we want to be the head, we still want to hold on to some of our things, some secrets. But be yourself. It's a big problem in the church, and we don't do so, it's as simple as God using a female to be the head instead. We shouldn't get any attitudes, but we need to get our attitudes right so that we can step in our proper positions and have teachable spirits. Many of us men don't have that teachable spirit and can't receive from one another, and I speak from experience. But I have no problem with that now because I want God to bless me, not just 50% or 75%, but 100%.

So Paul tells Timothy not to draw any personal fulfillment from the ministry, since that is not the issue. Rather, the call of God on our lives to be ministers of reconciliation and go to others is the issue. It's not about us feeling good, but it's about what God wants us to do. I have come to find that personal fulfillment and happiness are not the primary issues in my life, and it allows me to get up every morning and say, "God what do you want me to do today?" But I don't do everything that I feel that He wants me to do: I make bad decisions, I get myself into unnecessary debt, and sometimes I bypass people that I need to minister to because I think that something else is more important. As much as I love God, I can fall.

But when you stay focused on God and know that what He calls you to do is the main thing, you won't miss it because you will see everything that God wants you to see. You'll minister to every person that God wants you to minister to, though you don't have to preach a sermon to everybody. When we go to the crack houses and shooting galleries, all we do is feed the brothers, and pray for them and encourage them, because they've been preached to all their lives. It's easy for us to preach to people, but try loving them, try hugging a dirty prostitute or drug addict, so that they can really know that you love them. But I love hugging them, because I want to let them know that I am sincere and want them to sense the love of God that is in me. Sharing the love of God is the only thing that is going to win anybody over for the Savior, not how well we preach. The Holy Spirit does the convicting and when He convicts, He also convinces. That's His job, not ours.

Testimony of Purpose

In 2 Timothy 4:6-8, Paul gives his personal testimony to Timothy as an example of these five principles.

> *For I am already being poured out like a drink offering, and the time has come for my departure. I have fought the good fight, I have finished the race, I have kept the faith. Now there is in store for me the crown of righteousness, which the Lord, the righteous Judge, will award to me on that day— and not only to me, but also to all who have longed for his appearing.*

He talks about the life full of purpose, where everything he does is to please God. Even through the suffering, he took every stripe, every thrown rock, and every beating in the name of Jesus and embracing it. His life is coming to a close, and in essence, he gives his eulogy as he opens his heart to Timothy.

First, he says, "I have poured my life out for others. I gave others the same comfort and love that I received." If you know the story about Paul, he put a lot of people to death, but God changed the wretched man, turning his whole life around. God loved showing off, and while the world was saying that He couldn't do it, He said, "Watch this." So many people told me that I would never make it as a preacher, while I said, "Well fine, I just want to be used by God." But though they told me we wouldn't last in our little ministry, I'm still preaching the word of Jesus Christ, and our ministry is growing.

When the world doubts His word, He says, "Look at this- I am God, the One who hung the stars up in the sky, the One who molded man and breathed life into him." Remember, if you want to be blessed by God and used greatly, you've got to pour your life out for others. It's about others.

Secondly, Paul sought to be a model and never regretted it. The beatings he experienced were an example of what the Christians of his time were going to go through, but he said, "Timothy, don't worry about it." I tell you today don't worry about whatever you're going through now or will go through. You don't have to hang on the cross or have nails driven through you. But just remember that suffering and hardships bring maturity and healing into your life, drawing you closer to God. This is exactly what we need to develop character from the new creations that we are.

As a side note, as Paul sought to be an example, us men also need to be models. We need more godly men examples in the inner cities of America. All of our children want to be like the drug dealers with nice cars and jewelry. At Inner City Missions, we have a mentoring program for our kids, and we look for male mentors who can teach kids God's way. Take the kids to your offices and tell them, "There are other places besides your house, the store, and school." They don't know anything else outside of that little world, so they become drug dealers and addicts because that is all they see. We need to show them that there is a big world out there and they can be anything that they dream to be.

Thirdly, Paul fought the good fight and kept the faith. He said, "Brother Timothy, it's coming to an end. There are no more assignments for me, I have nothing else in me to pour out, and I have no more suffering to go through. It has all come to an end." Paul was a man of commitment. He lived a life of purpose, and you can too.

The Centurion's Amazing Faith

I believe faith is what we need to start out, whether we need a boost in faith, or the faith to make decisions about serving God. We cannot serve God sitting in the pew; we cannot fulfill the Great Commission of going out into our neighborhoods to reach the world by staying inside the four walls. Rather, we need to go out in the highways and byways and be able to tell our neighbors that Jesus loves them. I see so many people who go to church everyday, but everyday also bypass a homeless individual, an addict, or a prostitute. Every Sunday, you come to church and drive by somebody on the corner you know is lost, but can't take a moment to tell them, "Why don't you get in the car, let me take you to church. Or let me take you to get something to eat."

We all have a responsibility and I know sometimes, God cleans us up, but our flesh gets in the way. It's not about keeping the people happy, but about encouraging people and making them feel uncomfortable with where they are.

Luke 7:1-10 says,

When Jesus had finished saying all this in the hearing of the people he entered Capernaum. There was a centurion's servant, whom his master valued highly, was sick and about to die. The centurion heard of Jesus and sent some elders of the Jews to him, asking him to come and heal his servant. When they came to Jesus, they pleaded earnestly with him, "This man deserves to have you do this, because he loves our nation and has built our synagogue." So Jesus went with them.

He was not far from the house when the centurion sent friends to say to him: "Lord, don't trouble yourself, for I do not deserve to have you come under my roof. That is why I did not even consider myself worthy to come to you. But say the word, and my servant will be healed. For I myself am a man under authority, with soldiers under me. I tell this one, "Go, and he goes; and that one, 'Come,' and he comes, I say to my servant, 'Do this,' and he does it."

When Jesus heard this, he was amazed at him, and turning to the crowd following him, he said, "I tell you, I have not found such great faith even in Israel."

Now when Jesus heard about this individual He turned and told the crowd, "Look at this, not in all of Israel have I found such faith." Why would He say that? I've come to see that the crowd didn't have any faith to follow Him, because they were seeing things with their physical eyes. They were just following Him because there were some signs and wonders taking place. That's just like when we hop on the bandwagon at church because the church is growing, or the church is big on missions. That doesn't mean we are doing anything for missions.

Faith that Overcomes Frustration

But the faith of this centurion soldier is the kind that we need if we're going to be successful- faith to stop getting frustrated while in the mission field and doing ministry for the Lord, faith that amazed Jesus. It is faith that believes that no matter what kind of giant rises up against us, that the giant will come down, and no matter what mountain stands in our way of doing the Lord's work, it's got to come down in the name of Jesus.

I'm around missionaries all the time, and what I hear is frustration: there's not enough money coming in, we don't have enough laborers. But if Jesus' focus was only on the few uneducated men, and they got on His nerves because they did the opposite of what He was telling them to do, the disciples never would have grown. If He had said, "Father, I'm giving this up, uh huh, I ain't going there," He would have never died on the cross for us. But he didn't. If we are to amaze God with our faith, we need to have the same attitude like Jesus had, and still has. We need to forget about whether there are enough finances, and I'm speaking from experience, because I live from day to day by faith. I still don't have a salary, but I'm fine with that, because I'm not losing anything and I dress pretty well. I don't have enough laborers, with only a few volunteers here and there. But the one thing I can't say is, "Lord, forget this; let's close it down." Oh yes, there have been times in my secret place when I've cried out and I've said, "Lord I can't take this anymore. Lord, I can't keep getting all stressed out because my bills are like $8,000." But when I cry out, God just blesses us- a big check always comes in and we get the bills paid. So I learned to mature through that, and got to the point where I said, "Lord, here, it's yours. Let's focus on preaching the truth and reaching the people others don't want to mess with." The inner city is not a very good place to work- people prefer to go overseas. Nothing against overseas missions, but our Jerusalems are being forgotten.

I have a world vision. I visualize mission centers in Africa, Mexico, South America and a factory. People say I'm crazy, that we don't have any money, but I feel that this is from God. Three floors, 14,000 square feet used to disciple inner city people to train them to go to other parts of the world. To be able to bring mothers in with their children that the system said they had no room for, and teach them how to be moms again, whether they're single or not, and disciple men that the world has written off.

I myself was reached through a child, but my child was saved because of a missionary. And today, here's this missionary from the 'hood thinking of the world. We have to see it that way, but we can't make it happen if we stay inside the church, or run away from our neighborhoods. We can't make it happen if we don't befriend our neighbors, no matter what they're going through. They might be a wino, a drunk, but you don't know if that drunk will be a world missionary. He might be the one to raise up one of the largest churches in the city, and send out missionaries all over the world. And I'm a former drug addict that God already had a destiny for- because up to 1997, I told God, "No, Philadelphia is my Jerusalem, I'm staying here, I'm staying in the city because that's enough." But He said, "We're going to raise up people and continue to do this work, and I want you to go other places." I don't know how this vision of building mission centers in Africa and other parts of world is going to be fulfilled, but I've just been depending on God and being faithful to Him. If you don't know what to do, just be faithful, for He will direct your path, take you where you need to go, provide what you need to live off of, and raise up those who need to support you.

We can't serve God and be successful in serving Him if we don't have any faith. If we whine too much, it's not going to work. You're always going to get frustrated, but we need things to go bad while serving God, because that's what builds the character of Christ in us and strengthens us in our faith. Jesus says we will do greater works and greater things than He did. Why aren't we doing it? Why do we have to go overseas to see the miracles of God in action? We're always going around our neighborhood to go somewhere else. We can't neglect our neighborhood.

If we're going to grow in faith and see the Great Commission fulfilled through us, we need good examples to challenge us. The faith of this Centurion soldier is a perfect example of the kind of faith that we need, even for those who are discouraged and thinking of giving it all up. I'm telling you – stand. Keep pressing on, no matter how hard it gets, because God's going to turn it all around for you when you least expect it. That's the kind of faith that this Centurion had.

The Object of Our Devotion

Faith is stronger than mere belief. To believe is to simply have intellectual access to something. To have faith is to be inseparable from the object of our devotion. And who is the object of our devotion? Jesus Christ. And in Him is everything to fulfill the Great Commission. Our faith is who we are; we don't have anything as believers outside of that. Our intellect and our degrees aren't going to get it. You can hang up all the papers on your wall, but if you aren't fulfilling the Great Commission, you aren't doing anything. If you aren't ministering the gospel of Jesus Christ to somebody in the street, if you aren't telling somebody on your job about Him, you aren't doing anything. You can pay your tithes and come to all the Bible classes you want, but if you're not telling somebody about our Lord and Savior, you aren't doing anything. That's what it's all about.

It's time we stop playing games, time that we stop stroking people's egos for little things they are doing, and time to put our focus on the job that needs to be done. The stronger the faith of the believer, the stronger the assistant, and the more impact they're going to have. I want to go places and have people tell me that there is something different about me. What is it? We go places, people go past us, and we don't want to tell anyone. I love my wife, and my kids complain sometimes because she'll be in the supermarket, talking real loud about Jesus. How are they going to hear if somebody doesn't preach? We need to have impact on the world, and we can only do it by having faith in Jesus Christ.

What about this man's faith that caused Jesus to be amazed with him? It wasn't something that just happened. We aren't going to make it into the kingdom of God by just going along because some good things are happening. We need to be part of it, be in it, be directed by Christ. There are some principles about this man's faith that amazed Jesus that can help us become more faithful in our ministry to the world and our neighbors. I'm going to challenge you to say something to your neighbors, be nice to them, stop turning up your nose at them, or thinking that they're no good because they're alcoholic, or because they told you they don't want to go to church, because they might be the next missionary or pastor that touches hundreds of people.

The Faith of a Gentile

The centurion had faith that loved across barriers. That's one thing that still puzzles me about the kingdom of God. People call themselves servants of the living God, but there's still a lot of prejudice going on, and we're still looking down on one another. God doesn't see us as black, white, Hispanic, or Asian. He sees us all as His children.

That's what amazed Jesus about the centurion. Not only was he Gentile, but he was a soldier in the Roman army, which Jews hated, as they saw them as a corrupt force. However, the man was able to look beyond color and culture in caring for his servant. We give up too soon when we write people off without expectations. But the centurion officer didn't hold any grudges against the Jews because of their attitude towards him. Instead, he decided to love their God, because this God was the only one that could change the situation that he was in.

I could have gotten mad and cursed those who took the two tires off of my car but I prayed that the Lord bless them and send somebody their way. I could have easily built up hatred for them because they don't want God, but the god of this world has them blinded, and we're the only ones who can do something to get them to see the living hope Jesus Christ. But we can't give up.

The King James Version of Luke calls this unnamed man a certain centurion, a captain in charge of an often-corrupt force that could be quite brutal. Yet, the Gentile Roman soldier somehow loved his way through those who spit in his face. It takes faith when people come against you when you're doing the work of God. He looked beyond it all, across the valley and the obstacles that were in his way. He risked prejudice, rejection, misunderstanding- he risked it all. But he had faith and got excited about the work of God.

We may have hindrances, but we wouldn't be dependent on God if the enemy didn't put them in our way. The enemy is trying to do everything to keep us from reaching the world for the kingdom of God. I get excited about the work of God. I once heard a pastor say, "Give me a couple of prostitutes and a couple of junkies and I'm in Heaven," and I feel that way, because this work of God excites me. Too many of us are not excited enough, and church isn't cutting it.

This centurion was excited about the work of God, and said to himself, "I'm going to take a natural step of faith here because I know their living God is watching me," and went on to build the Jews a worship center. That's why the Jews went to Jesus and told him, "Hey, this man loves our nation. He even built us a beautiful worship center; you should see it. You got to go do this one." They were building the man up because he got excited about the work of God and built a place he wasn't even going to get an opportunity to worship in it.

Humble Faith

Matthew tells us in his account that the centurion's servant was lame and paralyzed, suffering great pain. There was a sense of urgency in the centurion's action, for he was really caring for a friend, not just a slave. He knew that Jesus Christ could heal him, and that is why he was able to look across the barriers. It is the same thing with us. If we're going to be successful in the mission field, we cannot see people as the world sees them. We look at them and get discouraged, thinking that there isn't any hope for them. We need to see them like God sees them- restored, standing on the rock of Jesus Christ, fulfilling the Great Commission.

There is so much persecution coming against our missionary brothers and sisters in all other parts of the world, while we in America don't realize how good we have it. Yet, we're still lazy. People are dying today, for the gospel of Jesus Christ. Can we say that we can do the same? They have no other choice because they know that He's the only hope for them, while all we see is our nice churches, jobs, and personal well-being. We need to repent. Start getting some excitement about the work of God. While others came to Jesus for selfish reasons, the centurion came for his servant.

How about if we start praying for those in need, giving to those who are risking their lives in other parts of the world for the gospel's sake, and deny ourselves? I love what Paul said in Philippians 2:3-4.

> *Do nothing for selfish or empty conceit, but with humility of mind let each of you regard one another as more important than himself. Do not merely look at your personal interest but also for the interest of others.*

Can we put somebody before ourselves? We have what we need to live a comfortable life and we want more. We want to keep up with the world, and we're losing our focus on living out the word of God, because we don't have any faith. It doesn't take faith for you to keep up with the Joneses, but it takes a lot of dying to the self to deny yourself to give others what we know.

When we do our annual Thanksgiving dinner for the children and the families, many parents don't want Christ. But we do not stop because they will come to Christ one day. The dinner is not just for kindness' sake, but is a way for us to fellowship and share the love of God with them. There are those who make sacrifices so that the church can take some Thanksgiving dinners to the crack houses and shooting galleries in North Philly. The elders may say, "Forget them junkies, they put themselves in that situation," but they're our neighbors. If we don't love our neighbors, we don't love ourselves. For every junkie, prostitute, and homeless person is my brother or my sister. I don't say this because I came out of that, but because it's what Christ says. If I say I love God and don't love my brother, something's wrong there- I don't love God.

The centurion had faith that understood and practiced humility. The Jewish elders built him up because he built them a synagogue; they were all pumped up and excited about and telling Jesus He should do the miracle for the man because of his previous deeds for us, but the centurion himself told Jesus that he was not even worthy of having him come under his roof. He had the faith to bring himself down, for he knew that if he humbled himself before God, God would do what he was asking.

If you humble yourself, God will do great things in your life. He might not send you, but He might give you enough to start giving and praying for those overseas. And if He builds up your faith, you're going to go. The centurion was accustomed to command, holding the power of life and death in his hands, and yet there was such contrast between him and the Jewish elders. They lifted him up because he built them a worship center, but he brought himself down.

Do we talk about what we got to do for missions because everybody else is doing it? Are we riding in excitement on somebody else's work or sacrifice? We need to stop hiding behind other people's visions, and line up with it.

Ultimate Confidence

Finally, the centurion had extraordinary faith and confidence in the power of Christ. He said, "Say the word, and I know my servant will be healed," and if he lived around here, I'm sure that he would have been in West Philly believing Jesus could just say the word in North Philly. It didn't take a lot of faith for the people in the crowd who were seeing Jesus work with their own eyes, but the centurion needed a lot of faith to believe that His word had power and authority to heal and deliver.

In the same way, we need to believe that His word has power and authority to provide whatever we need in the mission field or for our churches. All we have to say is, "Lord, just say the word, and I'll go, I'll do, I'll pray, I'll give." Do we have the extraordinary faith in Him that believes He is able to do abundantly more that we can ask of Him or even imagine? Even when we're down and we don't have anything, or when our physical eyes show us that there is no way we're going to make it from here to there, or even make it until tomorrow, do we have that extraordinary faith in Jesus to know that he'll come through for us?

I know from experience that too many of us focus too much on the problem instead of doing what God called us to do. He has already told us, "Seek my righteousness, do my work, do what I command you to do, and all these things will be added. Whatever you need, be it finances or food or labor, I'll take care of it. Just do what I told you." When we focus so much on the problem, we totally miss out on God's blessings. Now what I do is just kind of take my time saying, "Okay, we got a problem here Lord, it's in your court. I'm going to go to the crack house and the children's ministry, and I can't do anything else. Raised as the hustler I was, I can't even do anything for God." The Centurion betted everything he had on Jesus' power and authority, and today, each and every one of us have to do the same thing. We have to put everything we own and everything we are at the Master's feet. We want to be successful in reaching our neighbors, but they respond to us in a negative way because they can see through us. We might be church folks, but the world discerns better than us. But put all your attitudes and all your little perspectives about people at the Master's feet, and you'll see some responses and attitudes in your neighborhood that you've never seen before, or even imagined would be there.

Faith is able to move mountains, and it will move every one that stands in your way. Whatever you're going through, ask God to increase your faith and to help you search your heart. There might be some negativity in us that is keeping some of these mountains from being moved, and just because we're in the mission field doesn't mean that we don't have some issues we need to give to the Master. True faith makes a road where there is none. I know, for He's made a lot of roads for me, opened up a lot of windows and he's closed a lot of doors for me and for our ministry. I take no credit for it- I give my God all the glory and honor. I am privileged to serve with the King of Kings and the Lord of Lords, so much so that I tell people that

He trusted me, wretched man that I was. I was a drug dealer, a drug addict, a criminal that even cursed Him in his former life, but He entrusted me with His people and gave me a ministry, that I might fulfill the Great Commission.

It is the ability to seize the vision of our destiny with such a grip that it cannot be taken away until it's fulfilled. Whatever vision and desires God has given your heart to fill the Great Commission- hold onto it. Pray, humble yourself before God, because it cannot be pried out of your hands or loosened from the grasp of your spirit until it is completed.

Stepping Out for Jesus

A lot of people see Jesus causing the storm to be still as a mystery.

Mark 4:35-41 reads:

> That day when evening came, he said to his disciples, "Let us go over to the other side." Leaving the crowd behind, they took him along, just as he was, in the boat. There were also other boats with him. A furious storm came up, and the waves broke over the boat, so that it was nearly swamped. Jesus was in the stern, sleeping on a cushion. The disciples woke him and said to him, "Teacher, don't you care if we drown?"
>
> *He got up, rebuked the wind and said to the waves, "Quiet! Be still!" Then the wind died down and it was completely calm.*
>
> *He said to his disciples, "Why are you so afraid? Do you still have no faith?"*
>
> *They were terrified and asked each other, "Who is this? Even the wind and the waves obey him!"*

I have been to Israel, and I saw how easy it was for winds to come down and just pick up those waves. I can see why the disciples got scared, even with Jesus there, for the waves were terrible. We center our thoughts on the miracle that Jesus performed to calm the storm, but there is more knowledge here in these scriptures that we don't see. There are storms that rise up in our lives that cause us to just stay in the boat and be afraid to step out for Jesus Christ and be all that we can be for Him, but be encouraged. Here we see something of the vision of Jesus, for he said, "Let us go to the other side."

I've come to learn that Jesus was a calm individual and always knew what was waiting on the other side from studying this man and allowing the Holy Spirit to teach me. Even when they threatened to kill Him, He was calm. I would have probably reacted like Peter and wanted to chop off somebody's ears, but Jesus- He was calm throughout His ministry- nothing bugged Him, distracted Him, or caused Him to get off course. He knew that His course was chartered in life and what the end result was going to be. Nothing made Him take His focus off of what God the Father had ordained for Him. A lot of us here know our destiny, but sometimes we allow the storms of life to distract us. We need to forget about the storms of life and embrace them, because they are going to bring maturity in our lives and make us greater ministers for the Gospel of Jesus Christ.

Expectations of the Father's Plans

When Jesus said, "Let us go to the other side," there was a rest-lessness in Jesus' heart. Throughout His whole ministry, He knew what He had to do, as the Bible says He was always leaning on His understanding. He was leaning toward what was coming next, His mind not thinking on what happened before Him, who came against Him, or what He did, but on what was waiting for Him Ahead. We see that His whole life was always about moving from one place to another. He had to confront challenges all the time, because that's what kept Him going.

Today, we face challenges, and allow them to become obstacles to the fulfillment of God's perfect will for our lives. Everybody can accomplish more for the kingdom of God if we forget about these hindrances, for Jesus said in His word that we will do greater things than He did. Just because we've been living in the 20th and 21st centuries doesn't mean that this doesn't apply to us. If we put our faith in Him and give Him our all in all, we can meet those challenges. We can lay hands on the sick and they can be healed and we can confront hell and hell will have to back up because we're walking in authority and power- not of ourselves, but of Jesus Christ. When He went back to be with the Father, He said He would intercede for us and give us someone who would comfort us and empower us to do great and mighty things for Him. So we have the Holy Spirit.

The reason that we don't accomplish the great and mighty things that Jesus said we would is because we allow our own intellect and human abilities dictate what we need to do. It is easier to trust our own competence than the ability that God has given us through His spirit, because seeing it done with human ability doesn't take any faith. We just go on and do it because that's the way we learned how to do it. However, when we have to do it through the Holy Spirit's ability, it is a different story.

Jesus was moving from place to place, from challenge to challenge, always meeting needs. A lot of people say that meeting needs won't produce change, but that is the world's lie, because you never know when met needs are going to bring results. We are often more focused on seeing changes right away than on waiting on God to produce them- He is the changer, not us. All He said was that some of us sow, some of us water, while He gives the increase; but no, we insist on seeing changes produced right away.

I'm reminded of a young man I met who said, "Well, I'm a Catholic. I don't practice, I don't go to church or anything, but you know, I was baptized in the Catholic Church and all." So I ministered to him, and the young man accepted Jesus Christ that day. If I had been looking only to my human ability, I would have said, "Man, forget it, this guy is locked into this Catholic doctrine." There's nothing wrong with our Catholic brothers and sisters, and I've worked with a few of them who do believe in the blood of Jesus Christ and are not caught up in doctrine. But I feel so good, because today, he's a youth pastor in South Philly for a church that is part of the Assemblies of God, and every time I run into him, he always tells his companions, "This guy here led me to the Lord." It did so much for my spirit and motivated me, knowing that fruit was producing fruit.

The Need for More

I didn't get fat-headed, because God gets all the glory, but it encouraged me, because many of the drug addicts and prostitutes that I pray with and for every week accept Christ and are saved, but they just can't find their way out. They've been so deeply rooted in this addiction and bondage that they need somebody to be there for them on a consistent basis, to continue to hug them and encourage them. I came to find from experience that we can't just say, "Okay, say the Sinner's Prayer," and leave it at that. When I went to prison in 1989, I went in saved, and I continued to minister the gospel in prison and was on fire when I came home, wanting to do everything that God wanted me to do. I used to go feeding down Love Park and Center City, sharing my testimony and loving the people there. But I would get a sense that something was wrong, because the same individuals were saying the Sinner's Prayer every week. Then God dealt with me, and it was like He kicked the stool from underneath my seat, because He said, "Frank, it's more than just praying with them. You need to grab them by the hand and lead the way. Just like how the Holy Spirit leads the way for you." We can't just pray for these people and expect changes to take place. These people need to be nurtured with the love of Christ that is in us, and need to be encouraged that they can make it.

Jesus was meeting needs, and there is nothing wrong with meeting needs. Though the world says that the church is enabling people, it is a lie, because although they need the gospel, they also need to be fed and clothed. If you want to follow the commandments of Jesus Christ, look in Matthew 25. He tells us that if they're hungry, to give them something to eat; if they're thirsty, to give them something to drink; if they need clothes, to give them some; or if they're in prison, to go visit them. We aren't doing anything wrong, but who are we to judge that we're enabling them, and how are we ever going to win these people for Christ talking about Jesus all the time, while they're still telling you that they need a home, a job, or are still in addiction? We can't. Jesus met needs, and He didn't just minister to them spiritually, but also physically and emotionally. He touched them, healed them, and fed them. We ought to try some of that some time with our neighbor. Maybe like in the old movies - bake an apple pie and take it next door, and tell your neighbor, "I love you, I love you with the love of the Lord. There are no strings attached to this pie. I just want to tell you I love you." We probably need to take it a step further and say, "If I ever offended you, I apologize. If I came off as thinking that I was better than you because I go to church every week, I'm sorry." Then you will see some changes: you'll see that missionary in your neighbor when you bring them to church and get them discipled.

Going to the Other Side

People are searching, and we have what they need. We have the truth that will set them free, and yet we keep it to ourselves. That's why there are occults preaching to them, giving, and meeting their needs, and people are falling right into their trap, because we the church, who have everything they might need for them to live a productive life in Christ, won't give it to them. The horizon did not end where Jesus was at the moment. He knew that when He told them, "We're going over to the other side," that there would be a demon-possessed man who needed Him waiting there. You never know where you're going to go and who God is going to put in your face to tell them, "I love you, let me just give you a hug." We need to get this mindset together. We have a lot of theology and all the right answers, but we aren't walking in them. Something is wrong in the church.

But Jesus knew that it didn't stop right there when He got in that boat. He needed to rest for the simple fact that He knew that when He dealt with the demon-possessed man, He was going to be drained. He rebuked the disciples for being faithless and doubting Him. Jesus says, "Go, go into all the world and preach my gospel. Go to Africa, go to Korea." He sends us to these places and we say hear Him, and we go. And if God sends you, He will meet your needs. We don't have to worry about any harm, because the word says that He will make enemies at peace with you. It's like a young lady who found it hard to believe that there are Christians who actually minister to Muslims, and that there are missionaries that go to Islamic countries, risking their lives everyday.

Jesus knew that there were needs to be met on the other side, and He told those He helped to go and tell others of what the Lord had done. There are a lot of people waiting for us to meet their needs so that they, in turn, can go tell somebody else about not what you or I have done, but what the Lord has done. When we get people to understand what the Lord already accomplished on their behalf and also and what He will continue to do for them, we will see them become faithful disciples. Our faithfulness in Jesus Christ can do such things. When Peter and John healed the lame man who sat at the temple gate called Beautiful, it was their faith in Jesus Christ, not themselves, that empowered him to get up and walk in the name of Jesus. Everybody else, probably including many scribes and professors in those days, walked by and enabled him by putting money into his cup. However, though they had the education, they didn't have the connection to God. Just because we have a lot of Biblical information and theology doesn't mean we have a relationship with God. I speak to sinners everyday who know the Gospel better than I do, but their lives don't exhibit their words because they aren't walking what they're talking. That's why the Bible says it's better not to know Him, because a lot of us who do know Him are not doing His will.

I had a conversation with a young man who was highly educated, but didn't want Christ, though he knew the Bible and had grown up in church. I told him that I would rather know only a little bit of the word and be able to work it out than to know a lot and not do anything with it. It's not that I was putting the brother down, for I hated the sin in him, but I loved him. But just talking isn't going to get it because people are looking at you, and you are mocking God when you do not act. That is what the church is doing, too, since we are not exempt from it.

Stepping Out To Where God's Big Love Reaches
Jesus was not satisfied with settling down and concentrating only on a few people, and though we know that the twelve were His key disciples, Jesus' view was much bigger than that. His heart and His mindset were on the world, and that is why He told the disciples to go out into all the world and preach the gospel in Matthew 28:19. He said, "Go and make disciples of all nations; I don't care what they look like, I don't care what they're going through, just go and

make disciples of them." He didn't tell us to judge them or to worry about the problems we were going to face in the mission field. See, He knew that His purpose was to tell the world the truth about God, and that is also our own assignment at this service. And Jesus kept on moving to the next place and the next challenge.

Church, a lot of us are stuck in one place, inside the church. We've got to move to another place, where the sinners are at, where people have never heard of the gospel of Jesus Christ. I was offered one such opportunity while ministering to Korean students at a church in Michigan, when the pastor there asked if I would like to go to Peru with him to an area where some villages had never heard of the word of Jesus Christ. I got so excited in my spirit because that's where I wanted to go. I want to go where people have never heard the word of Jesus Christ, even when others avoid it because of the danger. We're still focusing on all the missionaries in the past that died, and already laid the groundwork for us. They already made the sacrifices for us. What are we waiting for? Why aren't we going over to the other side? Jesus Christ paid the price for us on Calvary, and the missionaries paid the price as they aged, died, even got skinned alive. Now these people are waiting for somebody to bring them the truth that they might be set free. But there is nobody to go over to the other side because the enemy still has a stronghold on our minds, telling us that the people are savages and that we will die if we go there.

I told God, "God, I want you to send me places nobody wants to go," and He started out by sending me back to my old neighborhood. For a minute, I asked, "Lord, why did you send me back here?" He sent me right back to where my drug addiction had started at the age of 11. Some of the brothers, now in their 40's, hide when they see me, and still call me Pastor Crazy, because that was my nickname back in the day– Crazy. I tell them that it's fine because I'm still me. I have been transformed by Jesus Christ, but I'm still me. He tested me if I was going to be faithful in the gospel by sending me right back to the hood. Now, God is moving me to other places, and I've developed a world vision. This is what this scripture is all about- the vision of Jesus Christ.

The passage of Mark 4:35-41 was about new challenges and new places, not crossing the river just for the sake of crossing. The disciples didn't see that, but Jesus knew, because He was always leaning on His understanding. We have to move outside of our walls, for we put God in a box. The Holy Spirit dwells in the church because it is where we worship Him and it is where His word comes forth and produces life in us, but we need to take what's been given here and apply it to our lives. Take it outside the walls, on to the other side, and apply it to the people that need it.

In Romans 10:14-15, Paul writes, "How, then, can they call on the one they have not believed in? And how can they believe in the one of whom they have not heard? And how can they hear without someone preaching to them? And how can they preach unless they are sent?" We are waiting on preachers, but everybody has an obligation, not an option, to preach the gospel of Jesus Christ. All Christians are ministers of reconciliation, reconciling the lost to Jesus Christ, the giver of life. You may not be in a pulpit every week, but you have an obligation to preach the gospel of Jesus Christ. If you do not do it, you are disobedient to God, and are sinning- and you wonder why nothing is happening in your life! Sin separates us from God- it's that simple. The people out there who are lost can't hear if we stay here just feeding off what the pastor, his staff, and all the Bible classes give us, because we're in here. We need to go out there, go to the other side. The words, "Let's go," must never be ignored in the body of Christ, but must always be a warning to us that we have to go wherever God sends us. We cannot argue with God, using excuses like, "I don't have a degree, I don't have experience." He is just asking for somebody who is willing to say, "Here I am Lord, send me." A lot of us should be in other places right now, ministering.

Going Ourselves

You might say, "Well, God didn't tell me I had to go there." Once you go there, you might find out what God can do with you. That's the problem today- a lot of us want to go where we feel comfortable, where there are no challenges and don't have to face any fears. We want to dictate to God. Instead of going to Africa, to Malawi or Nigeria where there is persecution taking place right now, we tell Him that we want to go to the suburbs. We don't want to go through the trials or the fire that's going to refine us that's in between the start and success of our ministry. Let go, and let God send you where He wants you. See if God is calling you to missions. We need prayer. But it is frustrating that people are praying more than doing. How much prayer time do we need to seeking God's face for an answer to what He wants us to do when it's right here? He said go; let's go over to the other side. He said go and make disciples of all nations. Do you believe it? It's right here. Then what do we have to pray about? If you're not working here, maybe you need to be overseas somewhere, or down in North Philly with me in the Badlands, instead of being home. Go over to the other side and get out of your comfort zone. The suburban churches are always in their comfortable zone, but it's not the truth. A lot of our Black and Hispanic and inner city churches are very comfortable. It's a dying world out there and we are comfortable and getting fat off the word.

The command to go should never be ignored by the body of Christ, but it needs to be a warning to us. Every time we turn around, we must heed that warning, and ask God, "Where do you want me to go? What do you want me to do?" I'm pretty sure that if you go to Africa, your mission committee will help you get there. People have to stop praying so much about things that we feel God wants us to do, and just do it. He will provide for you, He will take care of you. He says in His word that He's not a Father that will give you a serpent if you ask for a fish, or one that will give you stone if you ask for break. We serve a God that meets our needs, especially when we say, "Here I am, send me." He knows what you're going to need even before you get there.

People looked down on me, especially a lot of ministers, because I left my job a week before Thanksgiving. I was driving a truck; I was making $800 a week, but I felt He wanted me to leave it and step into this ministry and get it going. I told my wife a couple weeks before that, and she said, "Well, if He said it to you, He's got to say it to me; we're one." A week before Thanksgiving, my wife came to me and said, "Babe, God's confirmed it to me, you know I'll support you in it." She wasn't working at the time, but as soon as I left my job that New Years, the Lord blessed her with a job. The thing is here is that I didn't go into prayer, I felt the peace of God on my life a week before Thanksgiving. I didn't go raise support for a whole year before I did it, and I still don't. A few churches support us, but I never asked them to- God's going to take care of me, He knows what I need, and is all ready. There are those individuals that are going to support you financially and in prayer, and also those whose lives will be impacted by you. It's already in place- we just need to step over to the other side.

It's easy for people to become settled in their ministries. We need the committees, but we spend so much time trying to make decisions on what God wants us to do, that by the time we have a final decision, He's already passed us. He doesn't need us in that area anymore. We can get caught up in church and become stagnant, making us lose our focus on what God wants us to do. That causes us to be off focus of what God wants us to do. As followers of Jesus Christ, we must always be ready to step out of the boat, just like Peter. Peter didn't think about anything else, and when Jesus said to come, he came. He sunk when he looked at his human abilities- he probably was thinking that he shouldn't be walking on water. But when he was focused on Jesus, he was walking, walking towards the master. We too can walk towards Jesus, and He will lead us into the path that we need to go, to the people that we need to reach, and to accomplish the things that He wants done, but we need to keep our focus on Him. We cannot look at our circumstances, the amount of support, or the lack of people backing us up when we know that God has called us. Then you are being double-minded because you're saying that God can't do it for you.

We are either going to focus on God or on our problems. We are either going to do what God called us to do or we're not going to do it at all. Let's go back and get a regular job and be miserable all our lives. People ask if I ever think about going back to driving a truck, but I love what I'm doing. Even in the midst of my trials I've learned to laugh, for I can't do anything else. I can't go back and be on drugs. I'm saved now; I'm serving the Lord. If I go back to driving a truck, I'm not going to be happy because that's not what God called me to do. That was only for a season. We have to be always ready to go over to new possibilities in our lives in order to become productive and effective for the kingdom of God. There are so many possibilities out there in the kingdom of God that we must always be striving for them. We can't see them as human beings see them, but as God sees them. You can do it, you can go there. We cannot focus on persecution that is taking place; it's all over the world, and it has been happening since day one. We are no different today. But why try to prolong your life if you are going to be with Him anyways if you die in the midst of serving God faithfully?

Obedience to God's World Vision

Jesus had a vision to tell the world about God. Some of us don't have any vision and some of us don't know what our destiny is. We need to have vision in order for us to become productive kingdom servants. The Father's will is revealed in His word for everybody. If you take this to heart, you don't have to worry about your circumstances, about what you're going through, or where you need to be. Being a hearer of the word is not enough, but we have to become doers. Hearing isn't going to get it, even for missionaries. You can overcome any obstacles that come your way through Christ who strengthens you.

God is looking for people that He can raise up without fame and procession. God doesn't need boasters, but the humble, those who are not interested in titles. I understand we need to respect our pastors and our leaders, but it's not about the title. It's about us humbling ourselves before God and saying, "Here I am. Use me, send me. I'll stand in the gap and tell them which way to go." He's looking for those who will direct great events in history- telling the world that Jesus Christ is Lord; that Jesus Christ is the same yesterday, today, and for eternity; that Jesus Christ is the restorer, the deliverer, the healer, and the God of salvation. He's looking for people that can be given abilities to do certain things to do without question or reservation. The scripture is all about moving over to the other side.

Ways to Step Out for Jesus

I want to give three points because we can make a difference in our neighborhoods when we use our God-given designs and abilities. People will react different to us. God can't use us in Africa if we aren't willing to surrender and just humble ourselves before our local people here. I knew that God called me to ministry, but for seven years, I couldn't elevate myself, but had to line up behind another pastor's vision and support him. When I started humbling myself by submitting to that leader and his vision, God promoted me and said, "Okay, go start that ministry." But it took time- time of going through the fire and being refined, time of crying in my secret place, time on my knees and on my face. It took some sacrifices to get where I'm at, and it's going to take more to keep me where I'm going.

Vision is one of the most important aspects of stepping out. We must never be satisfied with where we're at. We must say, "I've been in Africa ten years, Lord, where do you want me to go next? How can I raise up local people here to take over the work so that I can go somewhere else, train somebody else, encourage somebody else?" That's what I'm doing. I'm praying that the Lord would send me to all those who are seen as no good, to the weak, the broken. Somehow, through the love of Jesus Christ in us, we can help bring restoration in their lives that they can take over this work. I don't want to import people; I want to raise up people from my own area, that they can be a testimony to the neighborhood. People can't receive from other people. How can you tell somebody about what they're going through if you've never been through it? How can you comfort a prostitute if you've never been a prostitute? We know Jesus knows. We need vision, and must never be satisfied with where we are.

Secondly, we must step out of the boat and go over to the other side. It takes faith to go over to the other side because you don't know what storm you are going to get caught in. But you need to trust God to get you over to the other side, so that you can do the work that is waiting for you. There is a dying world out there waiting, right in front our eyes, next door.

Thirdly, our desires must be righteous. We must let God's ways and will become engraved and grafted in our hearts.

Printed in the United States
77920LV00006B/733-762

9 781600 347337